ADDITION THE FUN WAY™

STUDENT WORKBOOK

© 1996

Key Publishers, Inc.
Sandy, Utah

ISBN 1-883841-36-4

Published in the USA

Written by: Judy Rodriguez
Illustrated by: Val Chadwick Bagley

ADDITION THE FUN WAY™

STUDENT WORKBOOK

For Information:
KEY PUBLISHERS, INC.,
6 SUNWOOD LANE
SANDY, UTAH 84092
1-801-572-1000

Copyright © 1996 by Key Publishers, Inc.
First Printing: 1996
Second Printing: 1997

ISBN 1-883841-36-4

Attention: Schools and Businesses
Addition The Fun Way Student Workbook is available at quantity discounts with bulk purchase for educational, business, or sales promotional use.

NOTE TO PARENTS AND TEACHERS

Addition The Fun Way is a picture and story method of learning the addition facts. It uses the same memorization techniques that are found in the highly successful *Times Tables The Fun Way* program. These include visualization, association, and mnemonics. *Addition The Fun Way* was developed in response to the abundant requests for an addition program similar to the *Times Tables The Fun Way* program. Students enjoy the variety and range of activities that are possible with the story method. Students will be practicing their reading <u>and</u> math skills while learning *Addition The Fun Way*. The Student Workbook should be used after teaching the appropriate pages in *Additon The Fun Way* Book for Kids (Student Text). The *Addition The Fun Way Teacher's* manual is designed for classroom or workshop use, (groups of 3 or more). The Teacher's Manual contains detailed lesson plans, games, game cards , and grading templates. Parents or teachers working one-on-one can teach the *Addition The Fun Way* program with the Book For Kids, Workbook, and Flash Cards. The *Addition The Fun Way* Flash Cards can be used to reinforce the story/number connection. Use the cards for review after each lesson. The lesson plan outline on page iv can be followed to assure that the ATFW Book For Kids stories are taught before the corresponding workbook pages are assigned. The lesson plan presents the stories in an order for most effective learning. After each lesson a game may be played to reinforce the facts presented.

The success of this method depends on adequate practice in applying the stories to the raw fact. Studies have shown that students who learn with the picture - story method retain the facts for longer periods and score higher on post-tests because the facts are firmly implanted in long term memory. In the early learning phases, it will be necessary to give story clues to students in order to trigger the answers to the facts. Once the stories are thoroughly learned and practiced with the workbook and text, students will by-pass the story when remembering the fact. So, the stories are an intermittent, but crucial phase of learning the addition facts by the picture and story method.

Parent involvement in a student's education has been shown to improve outcome. We applaud parents for taking an active part in their son or daughter's education. The rewards and benefits will pay off during the child's school years and beyond. Have fun teaching. We are sure that you and your student will enjoy learning *Addition The Fun Way*.

DESCRIPTION OF *ADDITION THE FUN WAY*
WORKBOOK MATERIALS

All About Me:

All About Me is a student questionnaire which serves as an icebreaker for students.   It starts the program with a personal and fun activity.

Pre-test:

The pre-test is timed for 6 minutes and used as a baseline to measure progress against the post-test. It contains 48 facts, some zeroes and all of the ones through nines, but no reversals, i.e. 7 + 4 but not 4 + 7.

Quizzes:

Quizzes are given at the start of each lesson. They are used to reinforce the stories by asking the students to draw a picture or write the story. This strengthens the connection between the story and the fact. If necessary, it is always better to review the stories or give hints during the quiz than to let the students leave the quiz section blank. Students learn by re-telling or drawing the picture of the story. The quiz has two parts. The upper portion is a test of the raw facts and the lower portion tests the student's memory of the stories. The story section should be marked correct if the students show any indication that they have remembered the correct story for that fact. Lesson 7 includes the Story Quiz. The results of the quiz should be used to determine the student's readiness for the post-test. If stories still need review, they should be reinforced by playing "Name That Story" or "The Pantomime Game."

Timed Practice Sheets:

These sheets are timed and used to practice the ones, twos, and nines. Students should write down the time it took them to complete the page. The goal is for students to improve their own times and scores on each type of Timed Practice Sheet. For example: The Ones and Twos Practice Sheet should get faster each time it is taken. However, the Nines Practice Sheet time should not be faster than the Ones and Twos because the Nines are harder. The Nines Practice Sheet Time should be faster than the last time the student took the Nines Practice Sheet.

Skill Practice Sheets:

The Skill Practice Sheets provide a graphic and interactive way to reinforce the introduced facts and stories. These include The Number People, Guess the Fact, and Match The Answer. All of the workbook sheets contain only the facts that have already been introduced. It is imperative to assign them in the order given. The Skill Practice Sheets are presented in a game-like format instead of rote repetition common to ordinary worksheets.

Learning Sheets:

These pages go through a step by step explanation of the new skill. Students will learn the subtraction facts by deleting or subtracting a picture from the story. Subtraction facts are taught after each set of addition facts is introduced. The learning sheets cover double digit addition and subtraction with and without regrouping, as well as adding nines, tens, and trios, (3 numbers). Some learning sheets are marked advanced. *These advanced learning sheets are optional. They can be given to those students who are ready for skills involving several steps.*

Activity Sheets:

These include: Help Bubba Find The Farm, Help Chichi Find The Bananas, Color The Baker, Color The Caveman, Fill In The Blank, Riddles and Mazes. These activity sheets reinforce the facts with story adventures, puzzle solving, and coloring. The activity sheets are recommended but they may be omitted if time is limited.

Crossword Puzzle: Facts are given as clues and students must fill in the key words of the story. This can be played in a group format or done individually.

DESCRIPTION OF WORKBOOK MATERIALS CONTINUED:

Post-test:

The post-test is timed for 6 minutes. The goal is for the students to score 100% on the post-test.

Stamp and Score Summary Sheet:

Students are able to map their progress by filling out their Quiz scores and Timed Practice scores and times. There is a square at the bottom of the sheet to put a stamp or a sticker when the indicated goals are reached. Students should be rewarded after each lesson for improving scores, receiving 100%, winning at the games, or completing workbook pages.

SKILLS COVERED IN THE STUDENT WORKBOOK

Addition Facts: 0 - 10

Subtraction Facts: 0 - 10

Double Digit Addition

Double Digit Addition With Regrouping

Double Digit Subtraction

Double Digit Subtraction With Regrouping

Adding Three Numbers In a Column (Trios)

DESCRIPTION OF *ADDITION THE FUN WAY* BOOK FOR KIDS

The Addition The Fun Way Book For Kids is in full color and printed on heavy, durable pages. The text covers the zeroes through the tens. All facts for the threes, fours, fives, sixes, sevens, and eights are taught with pictures and stories. Numerical tricks are used to teach the zeroes, ones, twos, and nines. Each fact is addressed once and not taught in reverse order. *Unlike the student workbook, which may be reproduced for classroom use, the pictures and stories in the Book For Kids may not be copied or reproduced.*

DESCRIPTION OF *ADDITION THE FUN WAY* FLASH CARDS

The flash cards are an integral part of the picture story method. The cards for the story facts show the number characters as well as the raw numbers. The characters with the numbers help the students transition from the story to the fact. The number at the bottom right corner of the card represents the lesson that the fact is introduced. The cards can be sorted and used in the order of presentation.

DESCRIPTION OF *ADDITION THE FUN WAY* POSTERS

The posters are useful for a classroom setting. They are in full color and printed on heavy stock with a durable coating. There are 22 posters size 13" x 19". Each story picture from *Addition The Fun Way* Book for Kids is enlarged with the caption beneath. The posters can be used as a visual aid while teaching the stories or posted in the classroom to enhance retention.

A WORD ABOUT MEMORIZING THE ADDITION FACTS

When students in 3rd, 4th, or 5th, grade need to stop and count with touch math or on their fingers to figure out the answer to an addition or subtraction procedure, they often become frustrated at the extra time it takes to do a simple problem. Unlike times tables, the fact is that many students can "get-by" without memorizing the addition facts. It is easy to count up or down to figure the answer. However, it is imperative that students have the addition facts memorized while doing problems with several steps like double digit multiplication, long division, or adding and subtracting fractions. Otherwise, students become lost in the counting procedures and forget which step is next. They are also more apt to make errors. The pictures and stories of *Addition The Fun Way* provide the context clues necessary for memorization. Students who have the addition facts memorized will have the tools to excel in future math encounters.

Addition The Fun Way!
LESSON PLAN OUTLINE

ADDITIONAL LEARNING ACTIVITIES

1. Ask students to make their own flashcards which illustrate the story. Make a new card each time a story is presented. **2.** Ask students to make their own books. They can use their imagination to illustrate the stories. They should always include the fact and the answer that goes with the story. Each time a new story is presented, ask the students to illustrate it in their book. **3.** Use the *ATFW* Picture Flash Cards to ask students to repeat the story in their own words. **4.** Sort the flash cards in sets of 10 or 12 and time students with each practice session. Students can try to beat their time on that particular group of cards. Cards are numbered with the lesson number on the bottom right corner. Use these numbers to sort and use the cards that have already been presented. **5.** Play the following games with the flash cards: Name That Story: Show a card. Student says one or two words from the story and the whole fact and answer. See how many can be done in 3 minutes. Try to beat the time. Pantomime Story Time: Student acts out the story while other players guess the fact.

Addition The Fun Way!

ALL ABOUT ME

1. What is your name?

_____

2. Do you have a nick name? What is it?

_____

3. Do you like school?

_____

4. In the box below, draw a picture of something you like in school.

5. What do you like to eat best of all?

_____

6. What do you want to be when you grow up?

_____

_____

7. How many people are in your family? Draw a picture of them in the box below.

8. In the box below, draw a picture of your pet or of your favorite animal.

AdditionTheFunWay!
Workbook - Lesson 1
PRE-TEST

# correct:	% score:
48	

NAME_____DATE_____TIME_____

7 +2	3 +2	5 +9	3 +6	7 +8	2 +6	1 +3	2 +4
3 +0	6 +4	7 +4	9 +4	1 +1	2 +2	5 +4	5 +2
3 +7	6 +9	8 +8	8 +9	4 +1	5 +5	6 +6	8 +6
9 +7	2 +8	9 +1	1 +5	0 +7	9 +3	6 +1	6 +7
7 +7	9 +9	3 +8	4 +4	4 +3	8 +1	2 +1	5 +3
8 +5	1 +7	2 +9	8 +4	5 +6	0 +9	3 +3	5 +7

AdditionTheFunWay!

Workbook Skill Practice Sheet - Lesson 1 Name:_____

THE NUMBER PEOPLE

Draw a line to the number person or thing.

7
5
4
6
3
8

Fill in the blank:

3 is a _____.

4 is a _____.

The 5 _____.

The 6 is _____.

7 is the__ ____ ____.

8 is a _____.

Draw a picture in the box for each number person or thing :

The 3-bee	The 4-door	The 5-drives
The 6 is sick.	The 7th Street Park	The 8-gate

AdditionTheFunWay!

Workbook - Lesson 1

ONES AND TWOS TIMED PRACTICE -1st Try

NAME_____DATE_____TIME_____

1 + 4	8 + 1	3 + 1	6 + 1
1 + 2	9 + 1	7 + 1	5 + 1
1 + 1	1 + 2	3 + 1	6 + 1
2 + 9	8 + 2	7 + 2	2 + 3
2 + 4	3 + 3	5 + 5	56 + 1

AdditionTheFunWay!

Workbook Skill Practice Sheet - Lesson 1 Name: _____
GUESS THE FACT

Directions: 1. Write the fact in the blanks below.
2. Write the answer to the fact.
3. Color the pictures.

Gee...I wonder if
we can figure this
one out...

_____ = _____
Fact   Answer

_____ = _____
Fact   Answer

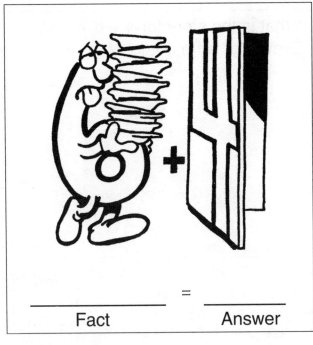

_____ = _____
Fact   Answer

_____ = _____
Fact   Answer

AdditionTheFunWay!
Workbook Lesson 2

QUIZ # 1   NAME_____DATE_____

Answer these facts:

$$3 + 3$$ $$5 + 5$$ $$3 + 7$$ $$4 + 6$$

CORRECT
_____
4

What is the story for 3 + 3 ?
Draw it or write it.

CORRECT
_____
1

What is the story for 5 + 5 ?
Draw it or write it.

CORRECT
_____
1

What is the story for 3 + 7 ?
Draw it or write it.

CORRECT
_____
1

What is the story for 4 + 6 ?
Draw it or write it.

CORRECT
_____
1

AdditionTheFunWay!

Workbook Skill Practice Sheet - Lesson 2   Name:_____
MATCH THE ANSWER

Directions:
1. Draw a line from the fact to the answer.
2. Write the whole fact and answer on the lines below.

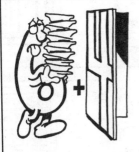

The 6 is sick.

10 Fix-It-Men

10 Fix-It-Men

14 "For the King"

Jumps over the 8-gate

10 Fix-It-Men

14 "For the King"

8-gate at the honey farm

AdditionTheFunWay!

Workbook Learning Sheet - Lesson 2   Name:_____

LEARNING SUBTRACTION - GUESS WHAT'S MISSING

Fill in the blanks:

$10 - \underline{\hspace{1cm}} = 5$

$10 - 5 = \underline{\hspace{1cm}}$

$5 + \underline{\hspace{1cm}} = 10$

$14 - \underline{\hspace{1cm}} = 6$

$14 - 6 = \underline{\hspace{1cm}}$

$6 + \underline{\hspace{1cm}} = 14$

$6 - \underline{\hspace{1cm}} = 3$

$6 - 3 = \underline{\hspace{1cm}}$

$\underline{\hspace{1cm}} + 3 = 6$

$10 - \underline{\hspace{1cm}} = 3$

$10 - 3 = \underline{\hspace{1cm}}$

$3 + \underline{\hspace{1cm}} = 10$

$10 - \underline{\hspace{1cm}} = 6$

$10 - 6 = \underline{\hspace{1cm}}$

$6 + \underline{\hspace{1cm}} = 10$

$14 - \underline{\hspace{1cm}} = 7$

$14 - 7 = \underline{\hspace{1cm}}$

$7 + \underline{\hspace{1cm}} = 14$

$8 - \underline{\hspace{1cm}} = 4$

$8 - 4 = \underline{\hspace{1cm}}$

$\underline{\hspace{1cm}} + 4 = 8$

$8 - \underline{\hspace{1cm}} = 5$

$8 - 5 = \underline{\hspace{1cm}}$

$5 + \underline{\hspace{1cm}} = 8$

AdditionTheFunWay!

Workbook Learning Sheet - Lesson 2 Name:_____
PURE SUBTRACTION - without pictures

Remember: The number on the top of a subtraction problem is the number person at the end of the story. Try to remember what the story is and then find the number person that is missing. That will be your answer to the subtraction problem. For example, the first problem is : $\begin{array}{r} 6 \\ -3 \end{array}$

Look at the problem, the 6 that is on top is the sick-six on the right of the picture after the = sign. The problem has a 3 in it. What is missing? The other 3-bee is missing. So 6 - 3 = 3. Can you do these?

Hints:	flower	crash	honey farm	snails	dishes	barn
	6	10	8	14	10	8
	-3	-5	-3	-8	-4	-4

Hints:	party	China	rocks	map	sisters	garden
	10	14	10	8	10	14
	-6	-7	-7	-5	-3	-6

AdditionTheFunWay!

Workbook Skill Practice Sheet - Lesson 2 Name:_____

GUESS THE FACT

I know it! I know it! Now what was that answer?

Directions:
1. Write the fact in the blanks below.
2. Write the answer to the fact.
3. Color the pictures.

_____ = _____
Fact   Answer

_____ = _____
Fact   Answer

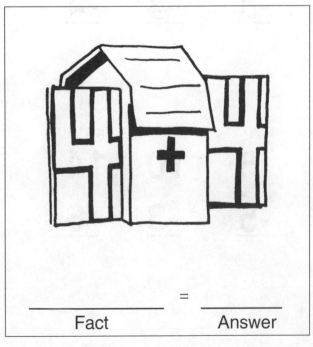

_____ = _____
Fact   Answer

_____ = _____
Fact   Answer

AdditionTheFunWay!

RUNNING INTO PROBLEMS

5 is trying to get home, but she keeps running into problems. Help 5 get home by solving the problem.

3 + 3 =

4 + 4 =

5 + 5 =

4 + 6 =

3 + 7 =

7 + 7 =

3 + 5 =

6 + 8 =

QUIZ # 2   NAME_____DATE_____

Answer these facts:

6	7	4	3	3	5	3	4
+8	+7	+4	+5	+3	+5	+7	+6

CORRECT
___
8

What is the story for 6 + 8 ?
Draw it or write it.

CORRECT
___
1

What is the story for 7 + 7 ?
Draw it or write it.

CORRECT
___
1

What is the story for 4 + 4 ?
Draw it or write it.

CORRECT
___
1

What is the story for 3 + 5 ?
Draw it or write it.

CORRECT
___
1

AdditionTheFunWay!

Workbook - Lesson 3

ONES AND TWOS TIMED PRACTICE - 2nd Try

NAME_____DATE_____TIME_____

1 + 4	8 + 1	3 + 1	6 + 1
1 + 2	9 + 1	7 + 1	5 + 1
1 + 1	1 + 2	3 + 1	6 + 1
2 + 9	8 + 2	7 + 2	2 + 3
2 + 4	3 + 3	5 + 5	56 + 1

AdditionTheFunWay!

Love Those Nines

Name:_____

Workbook Learning Sheet - Lesson 3
ADDING NINES

---

1. In the first space put a one.

Sample:

```
 9     4
+3    +9
 1     1
___   ___
```

2. In the second space put the number that is one less than the number that nine is added to:

Sample:

```
 9     4
+3    +9
12    13
___   ___
```

because 2 is one less than 3

because 3 is one less than 4

```
  9       9       9       9
 +6      +9      +7      +1
___     ___     ___     ___
```

```
  9       9       9       9
 +5      +2      +8      +4
___     ___     ___     ___
```

Page 14

AdditionTheFunWay!

Workbook Learning Sheet - Lesson 3   Name:_____
ADDING NINES *Page Two*

First, put a 1 in the first space of your answer. Next, put the number that is one less than the number that nine is added to. Be careful!! Sometimes the number that nine is added to is on top and sometimes it's on the bottom. Always use the number that is not the nine to figure out one less.

$$\begin{array}{c} 9 \\ +7 \\ \hline 1\ 6 \end{array} \qquad \begin{array}{c} 9 \\ +⑥ \\ \text{one less} \\ \hline 1\ ⑤ \\ 6-1=5 \end{array} \qquad \begin{array}{c} ③ \\ +9 \\ \text{one less} \\ \hline 1\ ② \\ 3-1=2 \end{array} \qquad \begin{array}{c} 9 \\ +2 \\ \hline \end{array} \qquad \begin{array}{c} 1 \\ +9 \\ \hline \end{array} \qquad \begin{array}{c} 8 \\ +9 \\ \hline \end{array} \qquad \begin{array}{c} 7 \\ +9 \\ \hline \end{array}$$

$$\begin{array}{c} 9 \\ +8 \\ \hline \end{array} \qquad \begin{array}{c} 9 \\ +1 \\ \hline \end{array} \qquad \begin{array}{c} 6 \\ +9 \\ \hline \end{array} \qquad \begin{array}{c} 9 \\ +9 \\ \hline \end{array} \qquad \begin{array}{c} 7 \\ +9 \\ \hline \end{array} \qquad \begin{array}{c} 9 \\ +5 \\ \hline \end{array} \qquad \begin{array}{c} 9 \\ +4 \\ \hline \end{array}$$

$$\begin{array}{c} 9 \\ +3 \\ \hline \end{array} \qquad \begin{array}{c} 9 \\ +6 \\ \hline \end{array} \qquad \begin{array}{c} 3 \\ +9 \\ \hline \end{array} \qquad \begin{array}{c} 2 \\ +9 \\ \hline \end{array} \qquad \begin{array}{c} 5 \\ +9 \\ \hline \end{array} \qquad \begin{array}{c} 9 \\ +2 \\ \hline \end{array} \qquad \begin{array}{c} 9 \\ +9 \\ \hline \end{array}$$

$$\begin{array}{c} 9 \\ +7 \\ \hline \end{array} \qquad \begin{array}{c} 8 \\ +9 \\ \hline \end{array} \qquad \begin{array}{c} 9 \\ +2 \\ \hline \end{array} \qquad \begin{array}{c} 9 \\ +4 \\ \hline \end{array} \qquad \begin{array}{c} 5 \\ +9 \\ \hline \end{array} \qquad \begin{array}{c} 9 \\ +9 \\ \hline \end{array} \qquad \begin{array}{c} 9 \\ +8 \\ \hline \end{array}$$

Congratulations! Now you know your nines!

AdditionTheFunWay!

Workbook Activity Sheet-Lesson 3

Turtle X-ing

A FEW LITTLE RIDDLES   Name:_____

Solve these riddles by answering the problems. Look for
your answer in the box below, then write it's partner word in
the blank. The first one is done for you.

How do turtles keep warm?

They   _____   _____   _____   _____

9+4   9+2   9+8   9+3   9+9

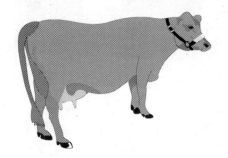

Do you know how long cows are milked?

_____   _____   _____   _____   _____

3+5   4+6   7+7   3+3   2+3

How do you measure a snake?

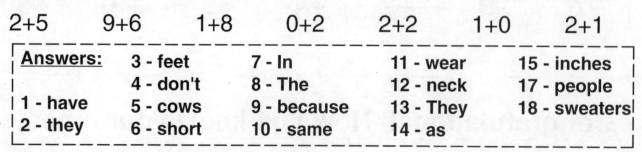

_____   _____   _____   _____   _____   _____   _____

2+5   9+6   1+8   0+2   2+2   1+0   2+1

Answers:	3 - feet	7 - In	11 - wear	15 - inches
	4 - don't	8 - The	12 - neck	17 - people
1 - have	5 - cows	9 - because	13 - They	18 - sweaters
2 - they	6 - short	10 - same	14 - as	

Page 16

Addition The Fun Way!

Workbook Skill Practice Sheet-Lesson 3   Name:_____

GUESS THE FACT

Directions:
1. Write the fact in the blanks below.
2. Write the answer to the fact.
3. Color the pictures.

Just can't wait to do this one!

_____ = _____
Fact   Answer

_____ = _____
Fact   Answer

_____ = _____
Fact   Answer

_____ = _____
Fact   Answer

AdditionTheFunWay!

Workbook Activity Sheet - Lesson 3

HELP CHICHI THE MONKEY FIND THE BANANAS

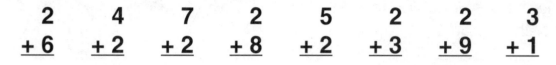

Name: _____

Step One: Fill in the answers to these facts:

2	4	7	2	5	2	2	3
+ 6	+ 2	+ 2	+ 8	+ 2	+ 3	+ 9	+ 1
___	___	___	___	___	___	___	___
Clue #1	Clue #2	Clue #3	Clue #4	Clue #5	Clue #6	Clue #7	Clue #8

Step Two: Match the answer for each clue with the picture and write the clue word in the blanks below.

10 - horse   4 - good-bye   6 - shark   11 - dragon

7 - bear   8 - island   5 - banana tree   9 - storms

1. The bananas are on an _____.

2. Ride the _____ to cross the bay.

3. Watch out for_____ along the way.

4. Take a _____ to the forest.

5. Talk to the _____.

6. Go to the _____.

7. Ask the _____ if you can have a bunch.

8. Say thank you and _____ to the dragon.

AdditionTheFunWay!

Workbook Skill Practice Sheet
Lesson 3 - Name:_____

WILLIE'S WORKSHEET-No picture adding

3	5	4	6	3	4
+4	+7	+8	+6	+5	+4

7	6	4	3	5	3
+7	+8	+6	+7	+5	+3

9	9	9	9	9	2
+4	+7	+8	+6	+5	+4

3	9	2	6	2	8
+2	+3	+9	+2	+5	+2

AdditionTheFunWay!
Workbook Lesson 4

QUIZ # 3 NAME_____ DATE_____

Answer these facts:

6	4	5	3	9	9	9	9
+6	+8	+7	+4	+3	+5	+7	+6

CORRECT
___
8

What is the story for 6 + 6 ?
Draw it or write it.

CORRECT
___
1

What is the story for 4 + 8 ?
Draw it or write it.

CORRECT
___
1

What is the story for 5 + 7 ?
Draw it or write it.

CORRECT
___
1

What is the story for 3 + 4 ?
Draw it or write it.

CORRECT
___
1

AdditionTheFunWay!

Workbook - Lesson 4

NINES TIMED PRACTICE - 1st Try

# correct:	% score:

$$\overline{20}$$

NAME_____DATE_____TIME_____

```
  9        8        4        9
+ 5      + 9      + 9      + 9

  3        6        9        9
+ 9      + 9      + 7      + 1

  2        9        5        9
+ 9      + 4      + 9      + 2

  9        9        7        9
+ 8      + 6      + 9      + 3

  4        5        6        6
+ 8      + 7      + 8      + 4
```

AdditionTheFunWay!

Workbook Learning Sheet - Lesson 4   Name:_____
LEARNING DOUBLE DIGIT ADDITION

Let's do one together and then you'll be able to do it yourself.

First, ask yourself what is 3 + 5?

(Remember, the 3-bee shows the 5-who-drives the way to the honey farm . She is at the.....)

```
  5 3
+ 1 5
    ?
```

Right! The answer is 8 because the honey farm is at the 8-gate. So, put the 8 right under the 5.

```
  5 3
+ 5 5
    8
```

Now ask yourself what is 5 + 5?

(Remember, the two 5's crash into each other and have to take their cars to the....)

```
  5 3
+ 5 5
  ? 8
```

Right, the answer is 10, because the 5's have to take their cars to the 10-Fix-It-Men. So write the 10 so the 0 is right under the 5.

```
   5 3
 + 5 5
 1 0 8
```

It is really important to learn to keep your numbers lined up in very neat columns. This will help you get the right answer when we learn to regroup in the next lesson.

Go on to the next page

Page 22

AdditionTheFunWay!

LEARNING DOUBLE DIGIT ADDITION *Page Two*

Now try this one yourself:

Ask yourself what is 3 + 3? Put your answer in the box:

```
  6|3
+ 8|3
```

Now ask yourself what is 6 + 8? Put your answer in the boxes to the left of your 6:

```
   6|3
 + 8|3
   |6
```

Good Job ! Now try these:

Hint: When there is nothing to add to the number, it's like adding 0, just bring the number down to the answer.

```
  3|5        4|3        7|5        3|4        2|5
+ 5|1      + 2|2      + 7|3      + 2|       + 2|
                                   3|6
```

You're doing great! Can you do these? Be sure to keep your columns straight.

```
   28        31        52        41        43
 +  1      + 33      + 73      + 84      +  2
```

LEARNING DOUBLE DIGIT ADDITION WITH REGROUPING

Let's do one together , and then you'll be able to do it yourself.

```
  5 4
+ 2 6
```

First, ask yourself what is 4 + 6?

Right! The answer is 10.

```
  5 4
+ 2 6
    ?
```

But there is only one column for the 10, so you have to squeeze the 1 into its waiting place......

```
    1
  5 4
+ 2 6
    0
```

Now ask yourself, what is 5 + 2? Right, the answer is 7, but before you write it you have to add the number in the waiting place, so ask yourself what is 7 + 1 ?

```
   1
  5 4
+ 2 6
  ? 0
```

Right, 7 + 1 is 8. Now you can write the answer in its column.

```
  5 4
+ 2 6
  8 0
```

Go on to the next page ☞

AdditionTheFunWay!

Workbook Learning Sheet - Lesson 4   Name:_____

LEARNING DOUBLE DIGIT ADDITION WITH REGROUPING *Page Two*

Now try this one:

Ask yourself what is 7 + 7? Write your answer:

$$\begin{array}{r} 6\,7 \\ +\ 4\,7 \\ \hline \end{array}$$

Now ask yourself what is 6 + 4?

$$\begin{array}{r} 6\,7 \\ +\ 4\,7 \\ \hline ? \end{array}$$

Ok, now keep the answer to 6 + 4 in your mind while you add the number from the waiting place.

Now write your answer.

$$\begin{array}{r} 6\,7 \\ +\ 4\,7 \\ \hline \end{array}$$

Good Job ! Now try these:

$$\begin{array}{r} 3\,3 \\ +\ 2\,7 \\ \hline \end{array}\qquad \begin{array}{r} 5\,5 \\ +\ 3\,7 \\ \hline \end{array}\qquad \begin{array}{r} 5\,7 \\ +\ 3\,7 \\ \hline \end{array}\qquad \begin{array}{r} 6\,6 \\ +\ 7\,7 \\ \hline \end{array}\qquad \begin{array}{r} 5\,5 \\ +\ 8\,8 \\ \hline \end{array}$$

AdditionTheFunWay!

ADVANCED SKILL   Name:_____

Another word for regrouping is carrying. Carrying isn't so bad.

Workbook Skill Practice Sheet - Lesson 4

REGROUPING IN ADDITION

36 +46	34 +58	45 +47	33 +37
47 +37	56 +38	44 +46	35 +35
48 +34	37 +55	46 +46	37 +43
38 +46	57 +37	36 +34	45 +45

AdditionTheFunWay!

Workbook Activity Sheet-Lesson 4   Name:_____

COLOR THE CAVEMAN

1. Find the answer for one problem on the caveman.
2. Use the color key to find the color for that section.
3. Color the section.
4. Repeat until the caveman is competely colored.

Color Key
6 = Pink
7 = Yellow
8 = Brown
9 = Red
10 = Blue
12 = Green
13 = Red
14 = Black

I want to be like you. Teach me to add by coloring me correctly.

3 + 4

4 + 6

8 + 1

5 + 5

7 + 7

3 + 3

7 + 2

3 + 6

6 + 8

4 + 8

TOE
5 + 8

3 + 5

5 + 7

TOE
6 + 7

4 + 4

AdditionTheFunWay!

Workbook Skill Practice Sheet-Lesson 4 Name: _____
GUESS THE FACT

Directions:
1. Write the fact in the blanks below.
2. Write the answer to the fact.
3. Color the pictures.

I wish we had *Addition The Fun Way* on Mars

_____ = _____
Fact   Answer

_____ = _____
Fact   Answer

_____ = _____
Fact   Answer

_____ = _____
Fact   Answer

AdditionTheFunWay!

Workbook Learning Sheet-Lesson 4   Name:_____
LEARNING SUBTRACTION - GUESS WHAT'S MISSING

Fill in the blanks:

12 - _____ = 6
12 - 6 = _____
6 + _____ = 12

12 - _____ = 8
12 - 8 = _____
_____ + 8 = 12

12 - _____ = 5
12 - 5 = _____
5 + _____ = 12

13 - _____ = 5
13 - 5 = _____
5 + _____ = 13

7 - _____ = 3
7 - 3 = _____
3 + _____ = 7

13 - _____ = 6
13 - 6 = _____
6 + _____ = 13

9 - _____ = 5
9 - 5 = _____
_____ + 5 = 9

9 - _____ = 6
9 - 6 = _____
_____ + 6 = 9

Page 29

Addition The Fun Way!

Workbook Learning Sheet - Lesson 4   Name:_____
PURE SUBTRACTION - without pictures

Remember: The number on the top of a subtraction problem is the number person at the end of the story. Try to remember what the story is and then ask yourself what number person is missing. That will be your answer to the subtraction problem. For example, the first problem is :
$$\begin{array}{r} 12 \\ -6 \\ \hline \end{array}$$

Ask yourself, what story ends with a 12 in it and has a 6 in it? It's the one with the 12 donuts that the 6's eat, there is a 6 missing. So, the answer to 12 - 6 is 6. Can you do these?

Hints:

donuts	flat tire	eggs	cook	storm	elephant
12	13	12	7	13	9
-6	-5	-8	-3	-6	-5

Hints:

rest	color	roses	bridge	breakfast	rain
9	12	12	13	7	13
-6	-4	-7	-8	-4	-7

AdditionTheFunWay!
Workbook Lesson 5

QUIZ # 4   NAME_____DATE_____

Answer these facts:

5	6	3	4	3	5	4	6
+ 8	+ 7	+ 6	+ 5	+ 4	+ 7	+ 8	+ 6

 # CORRECT

___
8

What is the story for 5 + 8 ?
Draw it or write it.

 # CORRECT

___
1

What is the story for 6 + 7 ?
Draw it or write it.

 # CORRECT

___
1

What is the story for 3 + 6 ?
Draw it or write it.

 # CORRECT

___
1

What is the story for 4 + 5 ?
Draw it or write it.

 # CORRECT

___
1

AdditionTheFunWay!

Workbook Lesson 5

ONES AND TWOS TIMED PRACTICE - 3rd Try

# correct:	% score:
$\dfrac{}{20}$	

NAME_____DATE_____TIME_____

1 + 4	8 + 1	3 + 1	6 + 1
1 + 2	9 + 1	7 + 1	5 + 1
1 + 1	1 + 2	3 + 1	6 + 1
2 + 9	8 + 2	7 + 2	2 + 3
2 + 4	3 + 3	5 + 5	56 + 1

AdditionTheFunWay!

Workbook Skill Practice Sheet-Lesson 5   Name:_____

MATCH THE ANSWER

Directions: 1. Draw a line from the fact to the answer.
2. Write the whole fact and answer on the lines below.

 **9-sign do not disturb**

 **13- friday the 13th**

 **12 roses for mom**

 **12 eggs to color**

 **home to the 7th Street Park**

 **9-sign for the zoo**

 **13- friday the 13th**

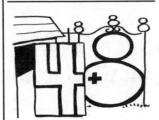 **12 donuts**

ADVANCED SKILL AdditionTheFunWay!

LEARNING SUBTRACTION WITH REGROUPING

When you want to subtract you look at the numbers and guess who is missing in the story. For example, 13 - 8 = ? 13 is the number at the end of the story and there is an 8-gate. Do you remember that? That's the story about the 5 who drives over the bridge and crosses the 8-gate on Friday the 13th. Who is missing in the story? Right! It's the 5-who-drives. So 13 - 8 = 5. Now try these.

$$\begin{array}{ccccc} 14 & 14 & 9 & 13 & 13 \\ -\ 6 & -\ 7 & -\ 5 & -\ 5 & -\ 7 \end{array}$$

Great Job! Now we will learn a new way to figure out subtraction problems with bigger numbers. What if you had this problem:

$$\begin{array}{r} 34 \\ -\ 6 \end{array}$$

First look at the two numbers on the right:

$$\begin{array}{r} 3\,|4| \\ -\ |6| \end{array}$$

The problem says 4 take away 6:

$$\begin{array}{r} 4 \\ -\ 6 \end{array}$$

Do you see that 6 is bigger than 4? If you had 4 apples and you tried to take away 6, you could not do that because you only have 4. So, you have to borrow some apples from

Go on to the next page ☞

your neighbor. This is how you do it:
The 3 is the neighbor next to the 4,
so borrow 1 from the 3. Cross it out
like this and change the 3 to a 2.
(Because 3 take away 1 is 2.)

$$\begin{array}{r} {}^{2}\cancel{3}\,4 \\ -\ 6 \end{array}$$

Now put the 1 that you
borrowed next to the 4 like this:

$$\begin{array}{r} {}^{2}\cancel{3}^{1}4 \\ -\ 6 \end{array}$$

Now you have 14 - 6 and that is 8, so
put the 8 below the 6 like this:

$$\begin{array}{r} {}^{2}\cancel{3}^{1}4 \\ -\ 6 \\ \hline 8 \end{array}$$

Now look at this part:
All you have is a 2, nothing
else to subtract,

$$\begin{array}{r} {}^{2}\cancel{3}^{1}4 \\ -\ 6 \\ \hline 8 \end{array}$$

so bring down the 2 and write it like this:

$$\begin{array}{r} {}^{2}\cancel{3}^{1}4 \\ -\ 6 \\ \hline 2\,8 \end{array}$$

The answer is 28.

Now try this one:

$$\begin{array}{r} 34 \\ -\ 8 \end{array}$$

Remember, you can't take 8 away from 4 because
the 8 is bigger, you have to borrow.

*Go on to the
next page*

☞

So, borrow a 1 frome the 3. Cross out the 3 and put a 2 next to it. Put the 1 you borrowed in the box next to the 4.

$$3\,4$$
$$-\,8$$

Now, ask yourself, what is 14 take away 8? *(snail story)*
Put your answer under the 8.

$$^2\cancel{3}\,^14$$
$$-\,8$$

Now bring down the 2.

$$^2\cancel{3}\,^14$$
$$-\,8$$
$$\overline{6}$$

Good Job!!

- -

Try these on your own.
There are story hints below the problem.

3 3	2 4	4 2	3 2	2 2
-7	-5	-5	-4	-6
Rainstorm	*no story*	*roses*	*eggs*	*donuts*

- -

3 4	2 4	3 0	4 0	2 0
-7	-6	-5	-5	-3
twins	*snails*	*crash cars*	*crash cars*	*sisters*

- -

AdditionTheFunWay!

ADVANCED SKILL Workbook

Skill Practice Sheet

Lesson 5   Name:_____

COOL! I can do these, where's my pencil?

PURE SUBTRACTION WITH REGROUPING-no pictures

storm

		flat tire	
43	33	43	33
-7	-6	-8	-5

roses

		eggs	
52	62	42	52
-5	-7	-4	-8

	snails		broken dishes
24	34	64	50
-7	-8	-6	-6

40	80	90	60
-4	-7	-3	-5

Addition The Fun Way!

Workbook Activity Sheet - Lesson 5   Name:_____

NUMBER GATE MAZE

Directions:
1. Start at the ☒
2. Trace your way through the maze to find the way out. Gates are marked by a ▮
3. You can crash through the gate only if you put the right answer down for the fact.

Don't be stuck in a maze.
Learn those addition facts!

5 + 6 =

3 + 8 =

4 + 7 =

3 + 6 =

4 + 5 =

4 + 8 =

5 + 7 =

6 + 8 =

6 + 3 =

I made it!

AdditionTheFunWay!

Workbook Learning Sheet - Lesson 5   Name:_____
ADDING THE TENS

Adding 10 to a number is easy. Take a look at this:

10 people   plus   3 people = 13 people

Do you see that 10 plus 3 is thirteen so 10 plus 6 must be 16. Write
your answers to the problems below. Do it like this:

Bring the 8 down   1 0   then bring the 1 down   1 0
                    + 8   + 8
                      8   1 8

Easy! The answer to 10 plus 8 is 18. Now do these:

10	10	10	10	10	10
+6	+5	+8	+3	+6	+5

10	10	10	10	10	10
+6	+4	+7	+8	+4	+7

AdditionTheFunWay!

# correct:	% score:
$\overline{20}$	

NAME_____DATE_____TIME_____

9 +5	8 +9	4 +9	9 +9
3 +9	6 +9	9 +7	9 +1
2 +9	9 +4	5 +9	9 +2
9 +8	9 +6	7 +9	9 +3
4 +8	5 +7	6 +8	6 +4

AdditionTheFunWay!

I love this book!

Addition The Fun Way

Name:_____

Workbook Skill Practice Sheet - Lesson 6
GUESS THE FACT

Directions: 1. Write the fact in the blanks below.
2. Write the answer to the fact.
3. Color the pictures.

_____ = _____
Fact · · · · · Answer

_____ = _____
Fact · · · · · Answer

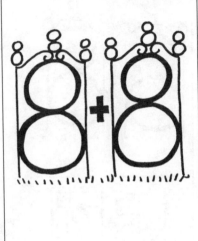

_____ = _____
Fact · · · · · Answer

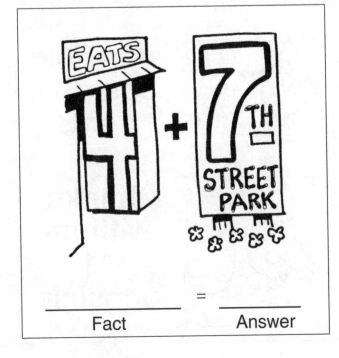

_____ = _____
Fact · · · · · Answer

_____ = _____
Fact · · · · · Answer

Addition The Fun Way!

Name:_____

Workbook Skill Practice Sheet - Lesson 6
MATCH THE ANSWER

Directions: 1. Draw a line from the fact to the answer.
2. Write the whole fact and answer on the lines below.

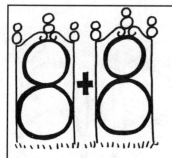 12 roses for mom

 storm on friday the 13th

 11 popsicle to cool off

 14 snails for the king

 must be 16 to drive

 11 popsicle costs 11 cents

 flag in 5's car makes 15

 thanks with an 11 popsicle

Addition The Fun Way!

Workbook Learning Sheet-Lesson 6   Name:_____

LEARNING SUBTRACTION - GUESS WHAT'S MISSING

Fill in the blanks:

11 - ____ = 3
11 - 3 = ____
3 + ____ = 11

16 - ____ = 8
16 - 8 = ____
8 + ____ = 16

11 - ____ = 7
11 - 7 = ____
____ + 7 = 11

14 - ____ = 7
14 - 7 = ____
7 + ____ = 14

11 - ____ = 6
11 - 6 = ____
6 + ____ = 11

12 - ____ = 8
12 - 8 = ____
____ + 8 = 12

15 - ____ = 7
15 - 7 = ____
7 + ____ = 15

9 - ____ = 3
9 - 3 = ____
3 + ____ = 9

Page 43

AdditionTheFunWay!

Workbook Learning Sheet - Lesson 6

Name: _____

PURE SUBTRACTION - without pictures

Remember: The number on the top of a subtraction problem is the number person at the end of the story. Try to remember what the story is and then find the number person is missing. That will be your answer to the subtraction problem. For example, the first problem is : $\begin{array}{r} 11 \\ -6 \end{array}$ Ask yourself,

what story ends with an 11 in it and has a 6 in it? That's the one about the sick-6 that goes to the store to get an 11 popsicle to cool off, there is the 5-who-drives that is missing. So, the answer to 11 - 6 is 5. Can you do these?

Hints:

caterpillar	drive test	snack bar	twins	hot head	store
11	16	11	14	11	12
-3	-8	-7	-7	-6	-8

Hints:

flag pole	hill	fence	popsicle	fever	eggs
15	9	11	11	11	12
-8	-3	-8	-4	-5	-4

AdditionTheFunWay!

Workbook Skill Practice Sheet - Lesson 6

Name:_____ **FILL IN THE BLANK**

6 + 6

Isn't that the one about the donuts?

Directions:
1. Fill in the blanks with the words listed below . Put a check mark by the word once you've used it.
2. Write the answer to the fact.

---

1. Two 6's are at the beach eating_____.
   (6 + 6 = _____)
2. The two 3-bees sting the 6 and make him_____.
   (3 + 3 = _____)
3. Two 5's crash their _____.
   (5 + 5 = _____)
4. The 3-bee stings the girls because they throw _____
   (7 + 3 = _____)
5. 6 plans a _____and smashes into the 4-door.
   (6 + 4 = _____)

__rocks   __cars   __sick   __party   __donuts

---

6. 6 gets sick at the 8-gate thinking about_____.
   (6 + 8 = _____)
7. The two 7th Street Parks are for the _____.
   (7 + 7 = _____)
8. Farmer John jumps over the 8-_____.
   (4 + 4 = _____)
9. The 3-bee shows 5 the way to the _____ farm.
   (3 + 5 = _____)
10.Jackie goes to the store to buy a dozen _____.
   (4 + 8 = _____)

__gate   __eggs   __snails   __honey   __king

AdditionTheFunWay!

Workbook Skill Practice Sheet - Lesson 6

Name:_____FILL IN THE BLANK pg. 2

8 + 8

Isn't that the one about the kid who gets his license?

Directions:
1. Fill in the blanks with the words listed below . Put a check mark by the word once you've used it.
2. Write the answer to the fact.

11. The 5 drives to the 7th Street Park to buy_____.
   (5 + 7 = _____)
12. 3-bee flies in the 4-door while Jeff is _____.
   (3 + 4 = ____)
13. 5 crosses the _____and gets a flat tire.
   (5 + 8 = _____)
14. 6 is at the park when it starts to _____.
   (6 + 7 = _____)
15. 6 is on the hill trying to _____.
   (3 + 6 = _____)

__cooking   __storm   __bridge   __rest __roses

16. 5 drives out the 4-door with an_____in her car.
   (5 + 4 = _____)
17. 6 is sick and needs a _____ to cool off.
   (6 + 5 = ____)
18. The 3-bee worked hard so the baby _____would be safe. (3 + 8 = _____)
19. Jim is happy because today is his _____.
   (8 + 8 = _____)
20. The snack _____has some delicious popsicles.
   (4 + 7 = _____)

__birthday __popsicle __bar __caterpillars __elephant

AdditionTheFunWay!
Workbook Activity Sheet - Lesson 6

Name:_____ SOLVE THE RIDDLE

Directions: 1. Work the problem below the blank line. Use your answer to find the word that goes with it. Put that word in the blank. The first one is done for you.

---

3 = raining   4 = careful   5 = step   7= poodle   8 = dogs

Why should you be ___careful___ when it's _____ cats

$5 + \underline{4} = 9$ $6 + \underline{} = 9$

$9 - \underline{4} = 5$ $9 - \underline{} = 6$

and _____ ? Because you might_____ in a _____.

$5 + \underline{} = 13$ $7 + \underline{} = 12$ $6 + \underline{} = 13$

$13 - \underline{} = 5$ $12 - \underline{} = 7$ $13 - \underline{} = 6$

---

4 = when   5 = ducks   6 = you   7= box   8 = quackers

What do _____ get _____ you put five _____

$6 + \underline{} = 12$ $3 + \underline{} = 7$ $3 + \underline{} = 8$

$12 - \underline{} = 6$ $7 - \underline{} = 3$ $8 - \underline{} = 3$

In a _____? A box of _____.

$7 + \underline{} = 14$ $4 + \underline{} = 12$

$14 - \underline{} = 7$ $12 - \underline{} = 4$

---

3 = snacks   4 = Pig   6 = wolves   7= favorite   8 = Newtons

What are _____ most _____ _____?

$4 + \underline{} = 10$ $3 + \underline{} = 10$ $3 + \underline{} = 6$

$10 - \underline{} = 4$ $10 - \underline{} = 3$ $6 - \underline{} = 3$

_____ _____.

$4 + \underline{} = 8$ $6 + \underline{} = 14$

$8 - \underline{} = 4$ $14 - \underline{} = 6$

AdditionTheFunWay!
WORKBOOK Lesson 7

QUIZ # 5 NAME_____DATE_____

Answer these facts:

5	4	3	7	8	5	6	5
$+6$	$+7$	$+8$	$+8$	$+8$	$+8$	$+7$	$+7$

#CORRECT
_____
8

What is the story for 5 + 6 ?
Draw it or write it.

CORRECT
_____
1

What is the story for 4 + 7 ?
Draw it or write it.

CORRECT
_____
1

What is the story for 3 + 8 ? Draw it or write it.

CORRECT
_____
1

What is the story for 7 + 8 ? Draw it or write it.

CORRECT
_____
1

What is the story for 8 + 8 ? Draw it or write it.

CORRECT
_____
1

AdditionTheFunWay!

Workbook Lesson 7   Name:_____
STORY QUIZ

DIRECTIONS:1. Write the answer to the fact.
2. Write the word that goes with the story .
3. Check off the word.

3 + 5 = _____	Story Word:_____	____caterpillar
3 + 4 = _____	Story Word:_____	____big flower
3 + 3 = _____	Story Word:_____	____honey farm
3 + 8 = _____	Story Word:_____	____breakfast
3 + 7 = _____	Story Word:_____	____rest on Hill
3 + 6 = _____	Story Word:_____	____Fix-It-Men

4 + 8 = _____	Story Word:_____	____party
4 + 5 = _____	Story Word:_____	____snack bar
4 + 4 = _____	Story Word:_____	____Bubba Bull
4 + 7 = _____	Story Word:_____	____eggs
4 + 6 = _____	Story Word:_____	____elephant

5 + 5 = _____	Story Word:_____	____flat tire
5 + 7 = _____	Story Word:_____	____Fix-It-Men
5 + 6 = _____	Story Word:_____	____donuts
5 + 8 = _____	Story Word:_____	____roses
6 + 6 = _____	Story Word:_____	____fever

6 + 8 = _____	Story Word:_____	____storm
6 + 7 = _____	Story Word:_____	____flag pole
7 + 7 = _____	Story Word:_____	____snails
7 + 8 = _____	Story Word:_____	____license
8 + 8 = _____	Story Word:_____	____twins

Addition The Fun Way!

Workbook Activity Sheet - Lesson 7

Name:_____

HELP BUBBA THE BULL FIND THE FARM

<u>Step One</u>: Fill in the answers to these facts:

8	5	4	7	6	5	6	3
+8	+4	+7	+8	+7	+7	+8	+7
___	___	___	___	___	___	___	___

Clue #1 Clue #2 Clue #3 Clue #4 Clue #5 Clue #6 Clue #7 Clue #8

<u>Step Two</u>: Match the answer for each clue with the picture and write the clue word in the blanks below.

15 - throwing   12 - helicopter   16 - China   9 - Bucky Bug

11 - balloon   10 - tractor   13 - post-card   14 - cowboy

1. Bubba is lost in _____.

2. Ask _____how to get back to Texas.

3. Ride a_____ across the ocean.

4. Land in Alaska, but watch out for kids_____balls.

5. Send a_____to Farmer John .

6. Ride a _____back to Texas.

7. Meet the _____and ask him for a ride.

8. Ride the _____back to your hay pile. Home Again!

ADVANCED SKILL

AdditionTheFunWay!

Workbook Skill Practice Sheet - Lesson 7

Name:_____

ADDITION WITH REGROUPING

Please take me to school so I can learn "Addition the Fun Way"

```
  48        57        55        44
 +38       +38       +47       +37


  57        46        43        34
 +37       +38       +48       +35


  45        27        36        43
 +36       +55       +66       +37


  38        56        46        25
 +45       +37       +54       +45
```

Page 51

Addition The Fun Way!

Workbook Learning Sheet - Lesson 7

Name:_____ADDING TRIOS

Example:

$$\begin{array}{r} 3 \\ 3 \\ +5 \end{array} = 8$$

First add the 5 + 3. If you remember that the 5 drives to the honey farm and the 3-bee shows the way at the 8-gate. Then you know the answer is 8.

Now add:

$$\begin{array}{r} 3 \\ 3 \\ +5 \end{array} \qquad \begin{array}{r} 3 \\ +8 \\ \hline 11 \end{array}$$

Now keep that 8 in your mind and add the other 3 to it. Remember that's the story about the caterpillar giving the 11-popsicle to the bee. So the answer to the trio is 11.

Can you do these?

$$\begin{array}{r} 6 \\ 7 \\ +2 \end{array} \qquad \begin{array}{r} 3 \\ 6 \\ +5 \end{array} \qquad \begin{array}{r} 4 \\ 5 \\ +3 \end{array} \qquad \begin{array}{r} 5 \\ 3 \\ +2 \end{array} \qquad \begin{array}{r} 3 \\ 6 \\ +7 \end{array} \qquad \begin{array}{r} 7 \\ 4 \\ +5 \end{array} \qquad \begin{array}{r} 6 \\ 5 \\ +4 \end{array}$$

$$\begin{array}{r} 8 \\ 8 \\ +3 \end{array} \qquad \begin{array}{r} 6 \\ 7 \\ +4 \end{array} \qquad \begin{array}{r} 5 \\ 5 \\ +2 \end{array} \qquad \begin{array}{r} 9 \\ 2 \\ +5 \end{array} \qquad \begin{array}{r} 3 \\ 5 \\ +4 \end{array} \qquad \begin{array}{r} 3 \\ 4 \\ +8 \end{array} \qquad \begin{array}{r} 2 \\ 1 \\ +9 \end{array}$$

$$\begin{array}{r} 9 \\ 6 \\ +3 \end{array} \qquad \begin{array}{r} 7 \\ 8 \\ +2 \end{array} \qquad \begin{array}{r} 4 \\ 5 \\ +1 \end{array} \qquad \begin{array}{r} 9 \\ 6 \\ +3 \end{array} \qquad \begin{array}{r} 3 \\ 7 \\ +2 \end{array} \qquad \begin{array}{r} 8 \\ 6 \\ +2 \end{array} \qquad \begin{array}{r} 7 \\ 3 \\ +8 \end{array}$$

Addition The Fun Way!

Workbook Activity Sheet - Lesson 7

Name:_____ **COLOR THE BAKER**

1. Find an answer on the baker. 2. Use the color key to find the color. 3. Color the section. 4. Repeat until the baker is colored.

Color Key

7 = any color
8 = brown
9 = black
10 = white
11 = pink
12 = blue
14 = green
15 = red
16 = orange
17 = yellow
18 = gray

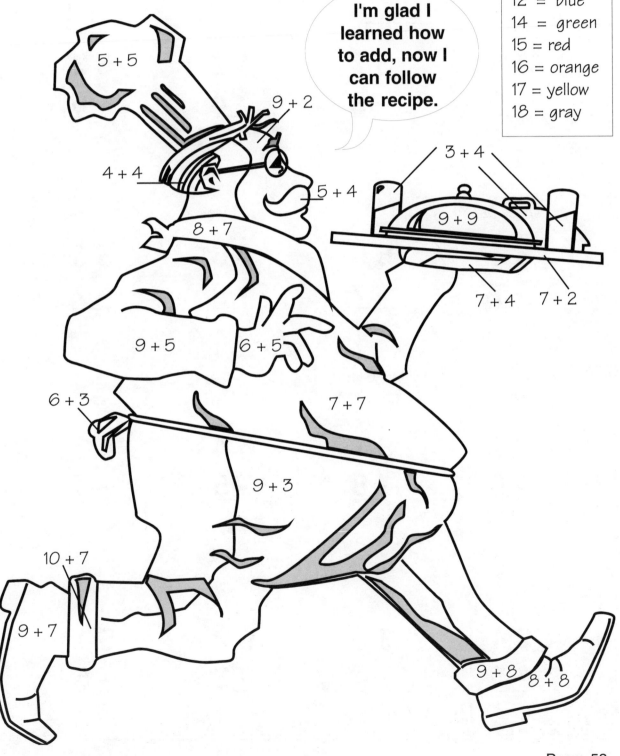

ADVANCED SKILL AdditionTheFunWay!

Workbook Skill Practice Sheet-Lesson 7

Name:_____

SUBTRACTION WITH REGROUPING

Can't wait until it's time for math..

snails		eggs	storm

snails
²3̶ ¹4
- 6
2 8

37
- 8

eggs
4 2
- 4

storm
5 3
- 6

snack bar
5 1
- 7

6 6
- 7

license
4 6
- 8

flag pole
5 5
- 7

fever
2 1
- 6

caterpillar
3 1
- 8

6 4
- 5

4 3
- 4

2 4
- 5

3 0
- 4

9 2
- 3

snails
6 1
- 5

AdditionTheFunWay!

# correct:	% score:
___ 20	

Workbook - Lesson 8
NINES TIMED PRACTICE - 3rd Try

NAME_____DATE_____TIME_____

$$
\begin{array}{r} 9 \\ +5 \\ \hline \end{array}
\qquad
\begin{array}{r} 8 \\ +9 \\ \hline \end{array}
\qquad
\begin{array}{r} 4 \\ +9 \\ \hline \end{array}
\qquad
\begin{array}{r} 9 \\ +9 \\ \hline \end{array}
$$

$$
\begin{array}{r} 3 \\ +9 \\ \hline \end{array}
\qquad
\begin{array}{r} 6 \\ +9 \\ \hline \end{array}
\qquad
\begin{array}{r} 9 \\ +7 \\ \hline \end{array}
\qquad
\begin{array}{r} 9 \\ +1 \\ \hline \end{array}
$$

$$
\begin{array}{r} 2 \\ +9 \\ \hline \end{array}
\qquad
\begin{array}{r} 9 \\ +4 \\ \hline \end{array}
\qquad
\begin{array}{r} 5 \\ +9 \\ \hline \end{array}
\qquad
\begin{array}{r} 9 \\ +2 \\ \hline \end{array}
$$

$$
\begin{array}{r} 9 \\ +8 \\ \hline \end{array}
\qquad
\begin{array}{r} 9 \\ +6 \\ \hline \end{array}
\qquad
\begin{array}{r} 7 \\ +9 \\ \hline \end{array}
\qquad
\begin{array}{r} 9 \\ +3 \\ \hline \end{array}
$$

$$
\begin{array}{r} 4 \\ +8 \\ \hline \end{array}
\qquad
\begin{array}{r} 5 \\ +7 \\ \hline \end{array}
\qquad
\begin{array}{r} 6 \\ +8 \\ \hline \end{array}
\qquad
\begin{array}{r} 6 \\ +4 \\ \hline \end{array}
$$

Page 55

Workbook Activity Sheet-Lesson 8   Name:_____

CROSSWORD PUZZLE

Across	Down
1. 3+7=10~3-bee gets mad and stings the _.	1. To get your driver's license you must be__.
2. If you have a dog, it is your _____.	2.5+6=11~5 drives 6 to the store to buy a__.
3. 3+5= 8~5 uses the map to drive to the_ _.	3. The ___Fix-It-Men
4. The 7 + 7 story is about twins from _____	4. 5+8=13~5's car gets a ___ ___.
5. 6+7=13~There is a_____ at the park.	5. 7+8=15~5 backs up with a __ __.
6. 3 + 3 is the story about two_____.	6. 5+7=12~5 wants to buy _____for mom.
7. 3+4=7~Jeff cooks _____.	7. To cry and cry and cry.
8. When 5 is with 5 they crash their _____.	8. 3+8=11~The popsicle is from Mrs. _____.
9. 4+5=9~5 drives out the 4-door with an___.	9. 6+6=12~The 6's get full eating _____.
10. Yesterday the hen_____ 2 eggs.	10. 4+4=8~Watch out for _____the bull.
11. 7+4=11~Take the 4-door to the _____.	11. 6+8=14~The king loves to eat _____.
12. Jackie goes to the store to buy _____.	12. There is a 5 who _____.
13. 3+6 =9~ The sign says Do Not_____.	

Addition The Fun Way!

Name:________________________

Workbook Activity Sheet - Lesson 8
3-BEE IS LOST IN THE HIVE

Directions: 1. Start at the ☒
2. Trace your way through the hive to help 3-bee find the way out. Gates are marked by a ■
3.You can crash through the gate only if you put the right answer down for the fact.

Help 3-bee find her way out of the bee-hive.

6 + 6 =
6 + 8 =
8 + 7 =
9 + 6 =
7 + 6 =
8 + 8 =
4 + 7 =
5 + 6 =
3 + 8 =
9 + 8 =
6 + 9 =
I made it!
Thanks for the help...

AdditionTheFunWay!

Workbook - Lesson 8 Name: _____

COMBINED SKILLS QUIZ

Addition

3	6	7
+ 4	+ 6	+ 8

9	7	8
+ 5	+ 6	+ 3

correct:
_____
6

Trios

4
6
+ 3

8
6
+ 4

9
3
+ 2

2
5
+ 9

correct:
_____
4

Subtraction

7	12	15
- 4	- 6	- 7

14	13	11
- 9	- 6	- 8

correct:
_____
6

Regrouping/addition

34	38	46
+ 6	+ 7	+ 5

67	25	53
+ 7	+ 8	+ 8

correct:
_____
6

Regrouping/subtraction

25	36	64
- 7	- 8	- 9

72	63	57
- 5	- 6	- 9

correct:
_____
6

Page 58

Addition The Fun Way!
Workbook - Lesson 8
POST-TEST

# correct:	% score:
48	

NAME_____DATE_____TIME_____

7	3	5	3	7	2	1	2
+2	+2	+9	+6	+8	+6	+3	+4

3	6	7	9	1	2	5	5
+0	+4	+4	+4	+1	+2	+4	+2

3	6	8	8	4	5	6	8
+7	+9	+8	+9	+1	+5	+6	+6

9	2	9	1	0	9	6	6
+7	+8	+1	+5	+7	+3	+1	+7

7	9	3	4	4	8	2	5
+7	+9	+8	+4	+3	+1	+1	+3

8	1	2	8	5	0	3	5
+5	+7	+9	+4	+6	+9	+3	+7

"ADDITION THE FUN WAY"
STAMP AND SCORE SUMMARY SHEET

Lesson 1

Pre-test
Score: _____
Time: _____

1's & 2's Practice
Score: _____
Time: _____

Stamps:

100% 1's & 2's	Question- naire pg.1	Number People pg. 3
Guess The Fact pg. 5	Won Game	

Lesson 2

Quiz # 1
Facts: _____ Stories: _____

Stamps:

Match The Answer pg. 7	Subtrac- tion pg. 8	Subtrac- tion pg. 9
Guess The Fact pg. 10	Run Into Prob. pg. 11	Won Game
Won Game		

Lesson 3

Quiz # 2
Facts: _____ Stories: _____

1's & 2's Practice
Score: _____
Time: _____

Stamps:

100% 1's & 2's	Improved Score 1's & 2"s	Improved Time 1's & 2's
Learning Nines pg. 14	Learning Nines pg. 15	Riddles pg. 16
Guess The Fact pg. 17	Willies pg. 18 Help ChiChi pg. 19	Won Game

Lesson 4

Quiz # 3
Facts: _____ Stories: _____

Nines Practice
Score: _____
Time: _____

Stamps:

100% Nines	Double Digits pg. 22 - 25	Regroup pg. 26
Color The Caveman pg. 27	Guess The Fact pg. 28	Subtrac- tion pg. 29 - 30
Won Game	Won Game	Won Game

Lesson 5

Quiz # 4
Facts: _____ Stories: _____

1's & 2's Practice
Score: _____
Time: _____

Stamps:

100% 1's & 2's	Improved Score 1's & 2's	Improved Time 1's & 2's
Match The Answer pg. 33	Regrouping/ Subtr. pg. 34-36	Regroup- ing/ Subtr. pg. 37-38
Learning 10's pg. 39	Won Game	

Lesson 6

Nines Practice
Score: _____
Time: _____

Stamps:

100% Nines	Improved Score Nines	Improved Time Nines
Guess The Fact pg. 41	Match The Answer pg. 42	Subtrac- tion pg. 43-44
Fill In The Blank pg. 45-46 Solve Riddle pg. 47	Won Game	Won Game

Lesson 7

Quiz # 5
Facts: _____ Stories: _____

Story Quiz
Facts: _____ Stories: _____

Stamps:

100%Story Quiz Stories	100%Story Quiz Facts	Help Bubba pg. 50
Regroup pg. 51	Trios pg. 52	Baker pg. 53
Subtr/ Regroup pg. 54	Won Game	Won Game

Lesson 8

Nines Practice
Score: _____
Time: _____

Combined Skills Quiz
Score: _____

Post-test
Score: _____
Time: _____

Stamps:

100% Nines	Improved Score Nines	Improved Time Nines
Cross- word pg. 56	3 Bee Lost pg. 57	100% Post-Test
	Won Game	

"ADDITION THE FUN WAY"
Workbook Answer Sheet

Pre-test/ Post-test Page 2, 59

9	5	14	9	15	8	4	6
3	10	11	13	2	4	9	7
10	15	16	17	5	10	12	14
16	10	10	6	7	12	7	13
14	18	11	8	7	9	3	8
13	8	11	12	11	9	6	12

The Number People Page 3

3 is a bee - 4 is a door - The 5 drives

The 6 is sick - 7 is the 7th Street Park

8 is a gate

Ones and Twos Page 4, 13, 32

5	9	4	7
3	10	8	6
2	3	4	7
11	10	9	5
6	6	10	57

Guess the Fact Page 5

3 + 3 = 6	3 + 7 = 10
6 + 4 = 10	5 + 5 = 10

Quiz # 1 Page 6

6	10	10	10
flower	crash		
rocks	dishes		

Match The Answer Page 7

6 + 4 = 10 Fix-It-Men   7 + 7 = 14,"for the King"

6 + 8 = 14, "for-the-king 3 + 7 = 10 Fix-It-Men

3 + 3 = The 6 is sick.5+3 =8-gate at honey farm

4+4 = jumps over the 8-gate 5+5=10 Fix-It-Men

Subtraction-Guess What's Missing Page 8

5, 5, 5	8, 8, 8
3, 3, 3	7, 7, 7
4, 4, 4	7, 7, 7
4, 4, 4	3, 3, 3

Pure Subtraction Page 9

3	5	5	6	6	4
4	7	3	3	7	8

Guess the Fact Page 10

6 + 8 = 14	7 + 7 = 14
4 + 4 = 8	5 + 3 = 8

Running Into Problems page 11

3 + 3 = 6, 4 + 4 = 8, 5 + 5 = 10, 3 + 7 = 10,

4 + 6 = 10, 7 + 7 = 14, 3 + 5 = 8, 6 + 8 = 14

Quiz # 2 Page 12

14	14	8	8	6	10	10	10
broken dishes		two parks					
Bubba the Bull		honey farm					

Adding Nines Page 14

15	18	16	10
14	11	17	13

Adding Nines page two Page 15

16	15	12	11	10	17	16
17	10	15	18	16	14	13
12	15	12	11	14	11	18
16	17	11	13	14	18	17

A Few Little Riddles Page 16

How do turtles keep warm?

They wear people neck sweaters.

13	11	17	12	18

Do you know how long cows are milked?

The same as short cows.

8	10	14	6	5

How do you measure a snake?

In inches because they don't have feet.

7	15	9	2	4	1	3

Guess the Fact Page 17

6 + 6 = 12	4 + 8 = 12
5 + 7 = 12	3 + 4 = 7

Help Chichi Find The Bananas Page 18

8	6	9	10	7	5	11	4

1. island	2. shark
3. storms	4. horse
5. bear	6. banana tree
7. dragon	8. good-bye

Willie's Worksheet Page 19

7	12	12	12	8	8
14	14	10	10	10	6
13	16	17	15	14	6
5	12	11	8	7	10

Quiz # 3   Page 20

12	12	12	7	12	14	16	15
donuts on beach			store, buy eggs				
roses for mom			cook breakfast				

Nines Timed Practice Page 21, 40, 55

14	17	13	18
12	15	16	10
11	13	14	11
17	15	16	12
12	12	14	10

Learning Double Digit Addition Page 23

6				
146				
86	65	148	36	27
29	64	125	125	45

"ADDITION THE FUN WAY"
Workbook Answer Sheet..continued page 2

Double Digit Addition-Regrouping Page 25

114				
60	92	94	143	143

Regrouping In Addition Page 26

82	92	92	70
84	94	90	70
82	92	92	80
84	94	70	90

Color The Caveman Page 27

3 + 4 = 7	4 + 6 = 10	5 + 5 = 10
7 + 7 = 14	3 + 3 = 6	7 + 2 = 9
3 + 6 = 9	8 + 1 = 9	6 + 8 = 14
3 + 5 = 8	5 + 8 = 13	6 + 7 = 13
4 + 4 = 8	5 + 7 = 12	4 + 8 = 12

Pink= face, Yellow=spear top, Brown=feet, Red=arms, Blue=spear, Green=bone, Red=toes Black=hair and shirt

Guess The Fact Page 28

4 + 5 = 9	3 + 6 = 9
5 + 8 = 13	6 + 7 = 13

Subtraction-Guess What's Missing Page 29

6, 6, 6	4, 4, 4
7, 7, 7	8, 8, 8
4, 4, 4	7, 7, 7
4, 4, 4	3, 3, 3

Pure Subtraction Page 30

6	8	4	4	7	4
3	8	5	5	3	6

Quiz # 4   Page 31

13	13	9	7	9	7	12	12	12

flat tire   storm at park
do not disturb   elephant

Match The Answer Page 33

5 + 7 = 12 roses for mom
6 + 3 = 9 sign do not disturb
6 + 7 = 13 - friday the 13th
3 + 4 = home to the 7-park
4 + 5 = 9 sign for the zoo
6 + 6 =12 donuts
5 + 8 = 13-friday the 13th
4 + 8 = 12 eggs to color

Subtraction With Regrouping -pg.1 Page 34

8	7	4	8	6

Subtraction With Regrouping -pg.3 Page 36

26	19	37	28	16
27	18	25	35	17

Pure Subtraction With Regrouping Page 37

36	37	35	28
47	55	38	44
17	26	58	44
36	73	87	55

Number Gate Maze Page 38

5 + 6 = 11	3 + 8 = 11	4 + 7 = 11
3 + 6 = 9	4 + 5 = 9	5 + 7 = 12
4 + 8 = 12	6 + 8 = 14	6 + 3 = 9

Adding The Tens Page 39

16	15	18	13	16	15
16	14	17	18	14	17

Guess The Fact Page 41

3 + 8 = 11	6 + 5 = 11	8 + 8 = 16
4 + 7 = 11	7 + 8 = 15	

Match The Answer Page 42

8 + 8 = must be 16 to drive
5 + 7 = 12 roses for mom
7 + 8 = flag in 5's car makes 15
4 + 7 = 11 popsicle costs 11 cents
3 + 8 = thanks with an 11 popsicle
6 + 7 = storm on friday the 13th
6 + 8 = 14 snails for the king.

Subtraction-Guess What's Missing Page 43

8, 8, 8	8, 8, 8
4, 4, 4	7, 7, 7
5, 5, 5	4, 4, 4
8, 8, 8	6, 6, 6

Pure Subtraction Page 44

8	8	4	7	5	4
7	6	3	7	6	8

Fill in the Blank Page 45 & 46

1. donuts	6 + 6 = 12	2. sick	3 + 3 = 6
3. cars	5 + 5 = 10	4. rocks	7 + 3 = 10
5. party	6 + 4 = 10	6. snails	6 + 8 = 14
7. king	7 + 7 = 14	8. gate	4 + 4 = 8
9. honey	3 + 5 = 8	10. eggs	4 + 8 = 12
11. roses	5 + 7 = 12	12.cooking	3 + 4 = 7
13. bridge	5 + 8 = 13	14. storm	6 + 7 = 13
15. rest	3 + 6 = 9	16.elephant	4 + 5 = 9
17. popsicle	6 + 5 = 11	18. caterpillar	3 + 8 =11
19. birthday	8 + 8 = 16	20. bar	4 + 7 = 11

Solve The Riddle Page 47

Why should you be (4)careful when it's (3)raining cats and dogs? Because you might (5)step in a (7)poodle.

"ADDITION THE FUN WAY"
Workbook Answer Sheet..continued page 3

Solve The Riddle Page 47 cont.

What do (6)you get (4)when you put five
(5)ducks in a (7)box? A box of (8)quackers.
What are (6)wolves most (7)favorite (3)snacks?
(4)Pig (8)Newtons

Quiz # 5 Page 48

11	11	11	15	16	13	13	12

hot head	snack bar	
caterpillar	flag pole	driving test

Story Quiz Page 49

3 + 5 = 8	honey farm
3 + 4 = 7	breakfast
3 + 3 = 6	big flower
3 + 8 = 11	caterpillar
3 + 7 = 10	Fix It Men
3 + 6 = 9	rest on hill
4 + 8 = 12	eggs
4 + 5 = 9	elephant
4 + 4 = 8	Bubba Bull
4 + 7 = 11	snack bar
4 + 6 = 10	party
5 + 5 = 10	Fix-It-Men
5 + 7 = 12	roses
5 + 6 = 11	fever
5 + 8 = 13	flat tire
6 + 6 = 12	donuts
6 + 8 = 14	snails
6 + 7 = 13	storm
7 + 7 = 14	twins
7 + 8 = 15	flag pole
8 + 8 = 16	license

Help Bubba The Bull Find The Farm Page 50

16	9	11	15	13	12	14	10

1. China	2. Bucky Bug
3. balloon	4. throwing snow
5. post-card	6. helicopter
7. cowboy	8. tractor

Addition With Regrouping Page 51

76	95	102	81
94	84	91	69
81	82	92	80
73	93	100	70

Adding Trios Page 52

15	14	12	10	16	16	15
19	17	12	16	12	15	12
18	17	10	18	12	16	18

Color The Baker Page 53

5 + 5 = 10	9 + 2 = 11	4 + 4 = 8
5 + 4 = 9	8 + 7 = 15	9 + 5 = 14
6 + 5 = 11	7 + 7 = 14	6 + 3 = 9
9 + 3 = 12	10 + 7 = 17	9 + 8 = 18
8 + 8 = 16	3 + 4 = 7	9 + 9 =18
7 + 4 = 11	7 + 2 = 9	

white = hat, brown = hair, pink = face & hands
black = mustache & tray, red = scarf,
green = shirt, blue = pants, yellow = cuffs,
orange = shoes, gray = cover

Subtraction With Regrouping Page 54

28	29	38	47
44	59	8	48
15	23	59	39
19	26	89	56

Crossword Puzzle Page 56

3 Bee Is Lost In The Hive Page 57

6 + 6 = 12	6 + 8 = 14	8 + 7 = 15
7 + 6 = 13	9 + 6 = 15	8 + 8 = 16
5 + 6 = 11	9 + 8 = 17	4 + 7 = 11
3 + 8 = 11	6 + 9 = 15	

Combined Skills Quiz Page 58

Addition:	7	12	15	
	14	13	11	
Trios:	13	18	14	16
Subtraction:	3	6	5	
	5	7	3	
Regrouping/Add.	40	45	51	
	74	33	61	
Regrouping/Sub.	18	28	54	
	67	57	48